W9-BBV-061

GEORGES ST-PIERRE

By John Hamilton

Published by ABDO Publishing Company, 8000 West 78th Street, Suite 310, Edina, MN 55439. Copyright ©2011 by Abdo Consulting Group, Inc. International copyrights reserved in all countries. No part of this book may be reproduced in any form without written permission from the publisher. A&D Xtreme™ is a trademark and logo of ABDO Publishing Company.

Printed in the United States of America, North Mankato, Minnesota.
052010
092010

PRINTED ON RECYCLED PAPER

Editor: Sue Hamilton
Graphic Design: John Hamilton
Cover Photo: Getty Images
Interior Photos: Ray Kasprowicz, p. 1, 3, 6-7, 8-9, 22-23, 24-25, 26 (inset), 26-27; AP Images, p. 2, 12, 13, 14-15, 16, 17, 30-31; Getty Images, p. 4-5, 10, 10 (inset), 11, 18-19, 20-21, 28-29, 29 (inset), 32.

Library of Congress Cataloging-in-Publication Data

Hamilton, John.
  Georges St-Pierre / John Hamilton.
    p. cm. -- (Xtreme UFC)
  Includes index.
  ISBN 978-1-61613-479-2
  1. St-Pierre, Georges, 1981---Juvenile literature. 2. Martial artists--Canada--Biography--Juvenile literature. I. Title.
  GV1113.S84 H36 2011
  796.8092--dc22
  [B]
                                 2010017906

CONTENTS

GEORGES

Georges St-Pierre is an Ultimate Fighting Championship (UFC) welterweight title holder. Most mixed martial arts fans agree that he is one of the best pound-for-pound athletes fighting in the Octagon today.

ST-PIERRE

On July 11, 2009, St-Pierre defended his welterweight title against number-one contender Thiago Alves. St-Pierre's stamina and skills helped him win the match.

FIGHTER

Name: Georges St-Pierre

Nicknames: Rush, GSP

Born: May 19, 1981, Montreal, Quebec, Canada

Height: 5 feet, 11 inches (1.8 m)

Weight: 170 pounds (77 kg)

Nationality: Canadian

Division: Welterweight—156 to 170 pounds (71 to 77 kg)

Reach: 76 inches (193 cm)

Fighting Style: Kyokushin karate, wrestling, Muay Thai kickboxing, Brazilian jiu-jitsu

Fighting Out Of: Montreal, Quebec, Canada

Martial Arts Rank: 3rd-degree black belt in Kyokushin karate, 1st-degree black belt in Brazilian jiu-jitsu

Mixed Martial Arts Record (as of April 2010)

Total Fights: 22

Wins: 20 (8 by knockout, 5 by submission, 7 by decision)

Losses: 2

STATS

Georges St-Pierre's UFC Fight Record

Event	Date	Result	Opponent	Method
UFC 111	3/27/2010	Win	Dan Hardy	Unanimous Decision
UFC 100	7/11/2009	Win	Thiago Alves	Unanimous Decision
UFC 94	1/31/2009	Win	BJ Penn	Technical Knockout
UFC 87	8/9/2008	Win	Jon Fitch	Unanimous Decision
UFC 83	4/19/2008	Win	Matt Serra	Technical Knockout
UFC 79	12/29/2007	Win	Matt Hughes	Submission
UFC 74	8/25/2007	Win	Josh Koscheck	Unanimous Decision
UFC 69	4/7/2007	Loss	Matt Serra	Technical Knockout
UFC 65	11/18/2006	Win	Matt Hughes	Technical Knockout
UFC 58	3/4/2006	Win	BJ Penn	Split Decision
UFC 56	11/19/2005	Win	Sean Sherk	Technical Knockout
UFC 54	8/20/2005	Win	Frank Trigg	Submission
UFC 52	4/16/2005	Win	Jason Miller	Unanimous Decision
UFC 50	10/22/2004	Loss	Matt Hughes	Submission
UFC 48	6/19/2004	Win	Jay Hieron	Technical Knockout
UFC 46	1/31/2004	Win	Karo Parisyan	Unanimous Decision

EARLY

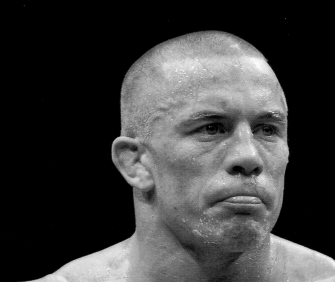

St-Pierre began learning Kyokushin karate at age 6. Later, he also learned wrestling, boxing, and Brazilian jiu-jitsu. St-Pierre first stepped into the Octagon at UFC 46 in 2004. He defeated Karo Parisyan in a unanimous decision.

Karo Parisyan

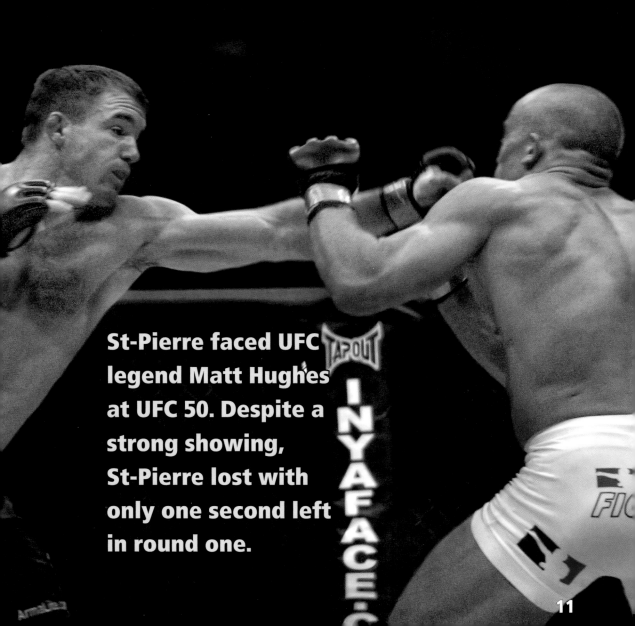

St-Pierre faced UFC legend Matt Hughes at UFC 50. Despite a strong showing, St-Pierre lost with only one second left in round one.

TRAINING

St-Pierre trains six days a week. He practices wrestling, jiu-jitsu, boxing, running, and strength training. He practices mixed martial arts sparring to prepare for UFC fights.

13

From 2005 to 2007, St-Pierre fought his way through the welterweight division. He won the UFC welterweight title at UFC 65 during a rematch with Matt Hughes. But at UFC 69, he lost a tough match against Matt Serra and lost the title. At UFC 79 on December 29, 2007, he fought Matt Hughes a third time. St-Pierre beat Hughes by submission in the second round.

Matt Hughes at UFC 79

14

Xtreme Fight

By beating Matt Hughes at UFC 79, St-Pierre became the new interim UFC welterweight champion. This set up a rematch with rival Matt Serra for the undisputed title.

UFC 83 Vs. Matt Serra

St-Pierre faced rival Matt Serra in a rematch in UFC 83 on April 19, 2008. The match was held in Montreal, Quebec, Canada, St-Pierre's hometown. After a flurry of takedowns and knee blows by St-Pierre, the fight was stopped in round two. St-Pierre had won back the championship title.

UFC 87 Vs. Jon Fitch

St-Pierre defended his title against Jon Fitch at UFC 87 on August 9, 2008. Fitch was a former Purdue University wrestling champ. But he was no match for St-Pierre's flurry of fists, elbows, and takedowns. St-Pierre won the match after five hard-fought rounds.

UFC 94 Vs. BJ Penn

At UFC 94 on January 31, 2009, former welterweight champ BJ Penn hoped to avenge an earlier loss against St-Pierre. During the first two rounds, St-Pierre had his hands full with Penn's elusive counterstrikes and takedown defense.

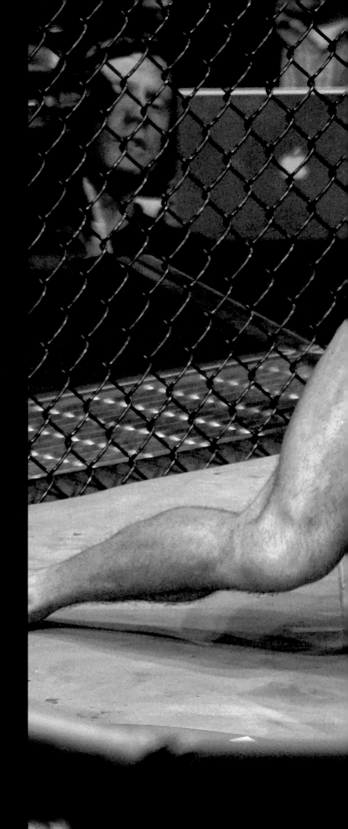

Ground and Pound

The final two rounds of UFC 94 were all St-Pierre. The champ started round three by scoring a "superman punch" against Penn. St-Pierre then punished the challenger with an aggressive "ground and pound" attack. The fight was stopped at the end of round four, with St-Pierre winning by technical knockout.

UFC 100 Vs. Thiago Alves

At UFC 100, on July 11, 2009, St-Pierre defended his welterweight title against Brazilian mixed martial artist Thiago Alves. In the early rounds of the fight, the powerful Alves showed excellent stand-up striking skills.

Injured, Bu[t]
Victorious

St-Pierre switched to a wrestling offense, repeatedly taking Alves to the mat. Alves escaped the takedowns, but he was no match for St-Pierre's endurance and ground control. St-Pierre won a unanimous decision, even though he tore a groin muscle during the hard-fought match.

UFC 111 Vs. Dan Hardy

At UFC 111 on March 27, 2010, Georges St-Pierre defended his title against scrappy English underdog Dan Hardy. St-Pierre won by unanimous decision.

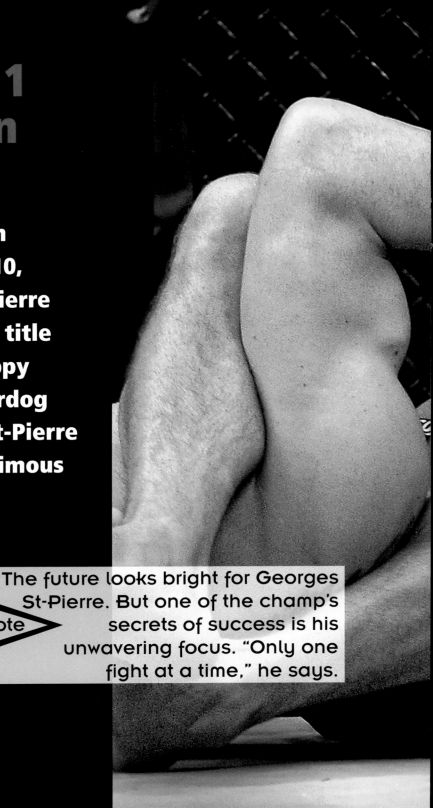

Xtreme Quote

The future looks bright for Georges St-Pierre. But one of the champ's secrets of success is his unwavering focus. "Only one fight at a time," he says.

Brazilian Jiu-Jitsu

A fighting style made popular by fighters from Brazil that specializes in grappling and ground fighting, including chokes and joint locks.

Decision

If a match finishes without a clear victor, either by knockout or submission, a panel of three judges decides the winner. If only two judges agree on the winner, it is called a split decision.

Ground and Pound

A style of fighting where an opponent is taken down and then punched or submitted.

Interim Title

A temporary championship title that is earned when the actual title holder can't fight, usually because of injury or illness. The interim title holder eventually fights the champion.

GLOSSARY

Kickboxing
A style of fighting that relies mainly on a mix of kicking and punching. Muay Thai is a type of kickboxing that is the national sport of Thailand.

Mixed Martial Arts
A full-contact sport that allows a mix of different martial arts, such as boxing, karate, and wrestling. The most popular mixed martial arts (MMA) organization is the Ultimate Fighting Championship (UFC).

Octagon
The eight-sided ring in which Ultimate Fighting Championship fighters compete.

Undisputed Title
When an injured or sick champion is healthy again, he fights the interim title holder. This determines who is the undisputed champion.

INDEX